Summary

Of

Keep Sharp
Build a Better Brain at Any Age

A book by
Dr. Sanjay Gupta

Content Created
By

Cosmic Publications

Note to readers

This is an unofficial summary of Dr. Sanjay Gupta's book "**Keep Sharp: Build a Better Brain at Any Age"** designed to enrich your reading experience. Buy the original book on Amazon.com

OUR FREE GIFT TO YOU

We understand that you didn't have to buy our summary, but because you did, we are very happy to give you something absolutely free.

Scan the QR Code to get free Access.

Table of Contents

Keep Sharp In A "Nutshell"

"Keep Sharp" by Sanjay Gupta details the various ways to address dementia and Alzheimer's before it becomes a problem. Gupta gives evidence of how Alzheimer's and dementia begins as early as the 30s, though evidence of this isn't present in someone's life until after they've reached middle-age.

In Part I, Gupta details how the brain and memory work. He dispels popular myths about the brain and memory, while also explaining how memories are encoded, the difference between short and long term memory, and how memory retrieval works.

In Part II, Gupta details the various ways you can make sure your memory stays strong into middle and older age, and if it already feels foggy, how to get it back to where you'd like it. With physical exercise, a good diet, adequate sleep, lifelong learning, and social connection, memory can be improved before it turns into a deeper problem.

In Part III, Gupta discusses how to handle a diagnosis of Alzheimer's. He further explains what it means, how a diagnosis is found, and how to best care for those who have been diagnoses. He gives practical advice on how to help yourself or family members who go through this disorder or other related disorders.

Gupta strongly believes that Alzheimer's and other dementia-related disorders are being studied voraciously and that there will be large scientific breakthroughs in the future.

Part One:
The Brain, Meet Your Inner Black Box

The brain is singularly the most important organ in your body. It is responsible for all functioning, and it takes 20% of the body's resources to do so. Neuroscientists are some of the most hard-working scientists because they must constantly study the high-functioning part of the body.

Chapter One:
What Makes You You

The brain is the most powerful organ in our body, though it weighs only three pounds. The brain is made up of millions of cells and synapses, all of which work together to input information into memory. Some have mistakenly likened the brain to a computer, believing it operates much the same way as a hard drive, but the truth is that the brain is even more remarkable. The brain is able to fill in missing gaps of data and ensure that information is processed steadily and accurately in a way that computers never could.

The brain is made up of many different parts, each of which functions differently and have specific uses. However, these parts are all interconnected, and learning the specific parts does not necessarily help you understand how the brain works.

The story of Phineas Gage is often used in psychology and neuroscience to explain and understand the brain. Gage was working on a railroad when he suffered an injury where a railroad spike went through his frontal lobe. Despite that, his functioning didn't change. However, his family and friends reported that his personality altered drastically, which allowed neuroscientists to hypothesize that perhaps the frontal lobe was the key part of the brain to understanding personality. Gage dies not long after due to seizures, but his friends and family did report that he started to act more "like himself" toward the end of his life, which is some evidence in the brain's ability to heal itself.

Often, when we think of memory, we think of memorizing. However, this isn't the way the brain or memory works. Memory is an intricate set of neural pathways that work together to make a picture of what an event was like. Our memory is constantly changing, each moment adding to it in an effort to make sense of what happened and to create a cohesive picture of what's going on.

Memories are also easily manipulated. In one study, a woman gave brochures to two groups of people who had recently been to Disney World. In some of the brochures, she placed a picture of Bugs Bunny. Many of the people who looked at these pictures "remembered" meeting Bugs Bunny—however, Bugs Bunny is not at Disney World because he's a Warner Bros. character. In this case, the brains of these people were filling in the gaps of their memory using the brochure, even though it wasn't accurate.

However, some memory feels almost automatic, such as singing a song you've known your entire life or driving a car. In order to improve memory function in your brain, we must work on all parts of brain function–those that you are conscious of and those that are automatic.

There are three main stages in building memory: encoding, storage, and retrieval.

Building A Memory´(Encoding)

Encoding is the process of creating a memory. All memory encoding begins with the senses. Your five senses tell your brain what information it's receiving and how to encode it into the brain. These pieces of information connect the hippocampus, where emotion is stored, to the frontal lobe through neural pathways, or synapses. As you pay attention to the world around you, you begin to create dendrites, which are tree-like structures in your brain that trench in deeply and allow you to create a stronger memory about procedural actions, thereby increasing your proficiency. Dendrites are the reason why you get better at an instrument or language when you practice every day, but if you take a week off, you may lose much of your progress.

Short-versus Long-Term Memory (Storage)

Everyone knows there are two types of memory, long-term memory and short-term memory. These two types of memory are stored in different places. Short-term memory is stored in the hippo-campus, and most people can only keep seven things in their short-term memory at one time, unless they find a way to break it up into smaller groupings (the way we do with phone numbers or social security numbers).

Long-term memory, however, is focused in the prefrontal cortex, and it allows for the complex memory we generally think of when we think of memory. This is where scenes from your childhood, songs, academic information, and other long-term memories are stored. This memory is unlimited, so we have to learn how to transfer short-term memory into long-term memory.

Retrieval

When people say they have a bad memory, what they really mean is they have poor memory retrieval. Memory retrieval is the process of recalling the things you have placed in memory. This is something you can work on improving.

KEY TAKEAWAY: The brain is an incredibly diverse and intricate organ that is the center of all our functions. Our short-term and long-term memories are both stored in the brain. The process of creating memories includes encoding, storage, and retrieval.

Chapter Two:
Cognitive Decline—Redefined

Most people assume cognitive decline begins in old age because that's where they begin to see the symptoms. The beginnings of cognitive decline look similar for most people: a fogginess in the brain, small mix-ups of familiar things, an increase in irritation and despondency, and a lack of social interaction. These are common steps in diagnosing someone with Alzheimer's or other memory problems.

However, the truth is that cognitive decline starts much earlier in life. In fact, even some 30-year-olds are experiencing the beginnings of cognitive decline. Instead of waiting until our fifties to begin paying attention to it, we should train younger people to spot it and prevent it.

Eight (Potential) Ways the Brain Begins to Break

Not everyone who is diagnosed with Alzheimer's is diagnosed with the same factors of Alzheimer's. There are eight different factors that can lead to degeneration of the brain.

The Amyloid Cascade Hypothesis (ACH)

The first factor is ACH (Amyloid Cascade Hypothesis). The brain needs amyloids and tau to function. It is part of what makes a healthy brain. However, some brains have too much of this protein and it digs deep inside brain cells and leads to build up of brain plaque. The natural mechanisms that are in place to repair DNA and brain cells can't keep up as we age, and this plague could affect memory.

However, when it comes to ACH, genetics also plays a part. Some families experience an unusual amount of plaque buildup but no adverse reactions, while others find plaque buildup that leads to early-onset dementia and early death. Genetics plays a key force in the role of Alzheimer's. Unfortunately, drugs that sought to reduce amyloid protein in the brain did not lead to a better outcome.

Tau and Tangles

The second is tau and tangles. Tau is also a protein in the brain that is needed to function, but too much of it can cause issues. In addition, tau can also be chemically changed in a way that is harmful to the brain. Tau is the protein that builds up in the brain when athletes are diagnosed with CTE, a brain issue that comes from head contact or trauma. It's this trauma that ends up affecting tau, causing it to take over the brain and dwarf functioning. It's essential to look at tau in the brain to understand Alzheimer's and cognitive decline. A buildup of tau is also the cause of mad cow disease.

Blood Flow

Those who have trouble getting blood flow to the brain also experience problems with memory function. This is because blood flow is needed to eliminate excess plaque. In addition, those who have poor blood flow to the brain are also significantly more likely to have problems with the blood brain barrier, a part of the brain that prevents toxic substances from entering the brain.

Metabolic Disorders

Metabolic issues also lead to cognitive decline. Those with increased weight around the abdomen, diabetes, or high blood sugar levels, lipid absorption problems (such as cholesterol) and hypertension are all more likely to develop cognitive issues as seniors. To this end, it's important that people take care of weight management when they're young.

Toxic Substances

Toxic substances also lead to a massive brain decline. In this case, toxic substances don't mean neurotoxins like lead or mercury, but whiffs of toxic chemicals we all encounter every day, such as pesticides. Research is still being done on how these chemicals affect the brain and memory within the brain.

Infections

Infections can also play a crucial part in the development of Alzheimer's and cognitive decline. This is because infections, such as Lyme disease, can sneak past the blood-brain barrier into the brain, wreaking havoc on our systems of operations. However, not everyone who gets an infection will have cognitive decline, and certainly not every type of cognitive decline is linked to an infection.

Rudy Tanzi's "Alzheimer's In A Dish"

Dr. Rudy Tanzi is famous for his experiment, "Alzheimer's in a Petri Dish", where he took brain cells and put them in a Petri dish, then exposed them to various factors to see how they reacted. The result was a stronger understanding of Alzheimer's and what affects the brain to behave disproportionately. Tanzi hypothesized that introducing amyloid blockers late was the real issue with the drugs, and that they needed to be introduced earlier.

Head Trauma and Injury

Head trauma and injury can also lead to memory decline. Studies have shown that professional athletes in sports like boxing, football, and soccer have greater cognitive decline than athletes in other sports, due to the trauma in the head.

Immune System Challenges and Chronic Inflammation

In addition to the other factors, inflammation in the body and brain can also lead to cognitive decline, as can the lack of an appropriate immune response. Keeping track of inflammation in mid-life, and even taking anti-inflammatory medicines like Advil or Tylenol can help reduce the risk of developing Alzheimer's.

Types of Cognitive Deficits

There are a few different types of cognitive decline.

Normal Aging

The brain begins to finish its work of maturing in the 20s, and then begins deteriorating in the 30s. This is due to a variety of factors, but mostly that the synapses in the brain are no longer as quick as they once were, and new brain cells take slower to form.

Mild Cognitive Impairment

Mild Cognitive Impairment (MCI) is a type of impairment that is mild. It's when someone forgets a name, but they can still function normally in the world. MCI is often the first stage for many Alzheimer's patients, however, that does not mean that all, or even most, people who experience MCI will also go on to experience Alzheimer's.

Dementia

Dementia is a very general term for the decline of memory function, but there are actually several types of dementia.

Vascular dementia is caused by a severe break or loss of blood to the brain. It looks like a silent stroke, which about half of all people with Alzheimer's have.

Dementia with Lewy Bodies (DLB) is when there is a buildup of Lewy bodies, a type of protein, in the brain. This affects the part of the brain responsible for cognition, movement, and behavior. It is this kind of dementia that's present in those with Parkinson's disease.

Front Temporal Lobe Dementia (FTLD) is a type of dementia that is triggered by gradual nerve cell loss in the front temporal lobe, which leads to changes in behavior like socially appropriate responses, loss of empathy or inhibition, poor judgment, etc. The changes in personality and behavior are the first signs of this form of dementia.

Alzheimer's disease is the most well-known form of dementia, and it is the kind of dementia that takes over and allows a person to forget basic functions, like driving or eating. It is progressive.

If someone has more than one kind of dementia at once, that is called 'mixed dementia".

Normal Versus not Normal

Often, people who experience trouble with memory worry because they don't know what normal memory lapses are versus abnormal memory. There are six types of normal memory lapses that shouldn't be of concern.

The first is absentmindedness, or the lack of original awareness. Absentmindedness isn't actually forgetting anything—it's a problem in the input process where your brain did to record what you did originally, so it cannot retrieve the information. If there is no awareness of the action, there can not be retrieval of it.

Blocking is also a normal memory issue that is not a cause for concern. This is when you try to access a memory, but it seems to be blocked, like your memory retrieval button is stuck.

Scrambling is another form of a normal memory problem. When scrambling, you forget little details, and then your Brian tires to make sense of it and does so incorrectly.

Fading away is another form of memory loss that should't worry you. This is when your older memories fade away to make room for newer ones. The brain is a use-it-or-lose-it type of organ, so when old memories aren't used it's normal and natural to let them fade away.

Struggling for retrieval is also very similar to absentmindedness. This is a problem with encoding information because you weren't paying enough attention at the time (such as forgetting someone's name because you didn't try to remember it). Still, very normal.

Muddled multitasking is the last of the memory issues that are normal. As you age, your ability to multitask decreases and the things you need to remember during sessions of multitasking are less likely to be stored in the brain.

Rethinking Cognitive Decline

Many people think Alzheimer's may be over-diagnosed, since so many patients seem to have it and it often accompanies normal aging. Many who are diagnosed with cognitive decline may have neither amyloid issues nor Alzheimer's.

Focus On Your Brain and Everything Else Will Follow

In order to change cognitive decline and set us up for brain success, we must begin focusing on the brain and how to take care of it.

KEY TAKEAWAY: Many people don't know what causes cognitive decline, or the different types of Alzheimer's. It's important to tell what is normal brain functioning and what is cause for concern.

Chapter Three:
12 Destructive Myths and the 5 Pillars That Will Build You

There are twelve myths about the brain that are repeated far and wide, but they need to be debunked. These myths are called the dirty dozen, and you need to know them to fully grasp how the brain works.

The Dirty Dozen

The first myth is that the brain is a complete mystery. This couldn't be further from the truth. The brain is one of the most studied organs in the body, but it is full of complexities. In order to truly understand how the brain works, one needs to study it in full. These scientists understand the way the brain works—it's not a mystery any longer to those who have studied it.

The second myth is that cognitive decline is inevitable as you age. This is a half-truth. Memory can certainly decrease as you age, and your brain cells do slow in production as you age—but they don't stop. Your brain is just as capable of memory when you are old as it is when you are young.

The third myth is that dementia is an inevitable part of old age, but we know this isn't true. Dementia is not normal aging.

The fourth myth is the old adage "you can't teach an old dog new tricks"—or that older people are unable to learn new things. This is patently false—even those with Alzheimer's disease can learn new things!

The fifth myth is that you must learn one language completely before you can master a new one. This is simply untrue. In fact, studies show that children who learn two languages at one time retain more of the language than those who do not.

The sixth myth is that if you have memory training, you'll never forget anything. This isn't true. Even those with memory training will forget things from time to time.

The seventh myth is that we only use 10% of our brains at one time. This isn't true, and doesn't make sense in an evolutionary way or logically. If we did not need 90% of our brains, we wouldn't still have huge brains, and we wouldn't think brain damage was such a tragic thing. The truth is that the brain is more like a town. 10-20% of it are the shops we go to that fire up activity, but the rest are the roads and neural pathways that connect the parts of the brain. This means all of our brain is essential because the brain is so complex everything is interconnected.

The eight myth is that there are brain differences between men and women that make certain genders more suitable for activities than others. This is false. These differences are more likely to be attributed to natural causes, socioeconomic factors, and personality. Women are more likely to develop Alzheimer's than men, but this is due to hormone fluctuation during pregnancy, not the brain itself.

The ninth myth is that doing a crossword puzzle (or other puzzles) each day can keep the brain doctor away, but this is also false. Puzzles only work one part of your brain at a time, so they will not keep you from developing issues in other areas.

The tenth myth is that you are either left-brain or right-brain dominant. This is a far-reaching myth, with many quizzes and tests designed to figure out which side of the brain you use most. While it's true that the right and left hemispheres of the brain have different functions, it's not true that one side dominates the other. Instead, they work together to make sure the brain works totally.

The eleventh myth is that you only have five senses: sight (opthalamoception), smell (olfacoception), taste (gustaoception), touch (tactioception), and hearing (audioception). The truth is that you have more senses than that. You also have the following senses: proprioception (a sense of where your body parts are), equilibrioception (a sense of balance), nociception (a sense of pain), thermoreception (a sense of temperature), chronoception (a sense of the passage of time), and interception (a sense of internal needs).

The twelfth myth is that you are born with the brain you'll have forever, and all your brain cells and neural synapses are present at birth. This is patently false. While your brain will not grow in size as you age, you are constantly making new brain cells and new neural pathways to connect parts of the brain. Scientists have found that we are creating new synapses, dendrites, and brain cells up until death. If this wasn't true, we would still have the same maturity we had during birth.

How To Keep A Sharp Mind

The five pillars of brain health, which will be discussed in the next part of this book, are: Move, Discover, Relax, Nourish, and Connect. In other words, exercise, discovery of new things, rest and relaxation, a healthy diet, and connection with others all lead to a healthy brain.

KEY TAKEAWAY: There are many misunderstandings about the brain and myths that have persisted. It's important to know the truth about the brain so we can embrace the five pillars of brain health.

Part Two:
The Brain Trust: How To Not Lose Your Mind

Chapter Four:
The Miracle of Movement

Exercise is the single greatest factor in how long you live, how healthy you are, and how your brain continues to work over time. If you only follow one pillar of brain health, make it be to exercise.

The Pact of Aging

Exercise is the only tool universally recommended for every form of dementia and age-related memory loss. Many of the drugs used to treat dementia only treat certain forms, or are ineffective as a whole. The FDA, however, has given universal approval to exercise as a way to help deal with Alzheimer's and other dementia-related memory loss.

It doesn't take as much exercise as you would think, either. Studies found that just 150 minutes of exercise a week, total, had a lasting impact on memory function. However, it does matter what kind of exercise you do. Mixing interval training and strength training is essential.

Smarter and Bigger Brains in Minutes of Movement

Exercise increases mental acuity in just a few minutes. It does so by increasing your metabolism, which helps your blood sugar regulate. When your blood circulation is flowing steadily, there is less sugar in your blood and your body can send more blood to your brain to increase functions. This allows for a jump in mental acuity unseen with any other remedy.

In fact, studies of primary and secondary school students have given us a lot of insight into how exercise affects intelligence and mental acuity. Across the board, students in schools where exercise has been lessened or eliminated have worst testing scores and do more poorly academically than students in schools that have more exercise incorporated into the day.

Moving Through Evolution

It's also important to look at our evolutionary origins and how our bodies and lives have changed since. As Homo sapiens, we were much more inclined to exercise. In fact, survival was dependent on exercise as hunter-gatherers. However, as society flourished and there was less need to hunt and gather our own food, we became more sedentary and our bodies still haven't caught up.

Shape Your Brain By Getting In Shape

Exercise has long been believed to help our bodies in many ways. It not only increases mental acuity by increasing blood flow to the brain, but it also combats cortisol, the key hormone in stress responses. Cortisol is the culprit for bad health in children with stressful home lives and abusive situations. It makes the blood sugar problem worse! However, exercise has been shown to reduce cortisol levels and help lower stress, thereby doubling the effect exercise has on mental acuity by increasing blood flow and eliminating toxicity from the blood.

Research has also found that higher aerobic fitness levels leads to stronger white matter in the brain, as well as a lower risk of hypertension (high blood pressure). This is significant, as both high blood pressure and weak white matter in the brain are warning signs for dementia and other cognitive declines.

Just as You Would Brush Your Teeth

We need to begin to treat exercise the same way we would brushing our teeth, by making it a necessary and non-negotiable every day habit. When we talk about exercise, we aren't just talking about "working out" as people colloquially call it, but also about physical activity throughout the day where a sedentary lifestyle may be more common—things like taking the stairs instead of the elevator, etc.

KEY TAKEAWAY: Exercise and physical activity is the leading factor in preventing significant cognitive decline.

Chapter Five:
The Power of Purpose, Learning, and Discovery

Scientists have found that for each year you work, your risk of developing dementia goes down by 3.2 percent. This is because work keeps you physically and socially active, and it engages your mind. The people in Okinawa, Japan, look at aging as a chance to try new things—not as a chance to stop living and relax. Japanese elders are consistently learning and discovering new things about themselves and their hobbies.

Keeping the Brain Plastic

Cognitive reserve, or how you are able to keep your brain flexible, is a huge factor in brain health. People who have cognitive reserve are better able to overcome many different ailments, as opposed to those who do not. Cognitive reserve is made up of the changes to your brain as you try new things and create more synapses.

The Brain and Cognitive Reserve

Think of cognitive reserve in the same vein as the town analogy from earlier. If the brain is a town, and the synapses are the roads between the big centers, cognitive reserve is how well you are able to drive on the roads when foreign objects enter the scene. When stress or trauma runs the red light, your level of cognitive reserve is what enables you to swerve out of danger. It is the mechanism that keeps you flexible and able to bend away from problems.

There have been many studies that show higher education leads to greater mental acuity than people who don't have higher education. This is somewhat true and somewhat false. The truth is that it doesn't matter where you got a degree, or even if you got a degree. What matters for building mental acuity and cognitive reserves is that you are constantly learning and discovering new things. Those who invest in lifelong education, by picking up a book from the library or doing a crossword puzzle, invest in a sharper brain with more new synapses and strengthened old ones. This enables them to have a greater cognitive reserve, and to be able to steer around obstacles to mental clarity, such as dementia.

The Definition of "Cognitively Stimulating" Activities

The type of cognitive memory-enhancing you do is also essential. While puzzles and games may help keep your short-term memory up to par, there are two types of cognitive learning and discovery that will do even more for your brain than those.
The first is to take a class. The reason you should take a class is not only because it's informative and fun, with a social aspect, but also because it requires depth and complexity. Classes require you to focus, retain information both short and long term, and think critically

and solve problems. These are some of the key elements to maintaining cognitive reserve and have been shown to lower the risk of Alzheimer's by almost 30%.

The second is to play speed games. You may remember a speed game from your childhood—Punch Buggy. This game involved scanning the roads for Volkswagen Bugs, then punching the other player once you saw one. The game was simple enough, but it used quite a bit of your brain. The first thing it did was taught you to focus on a large scale by teaching you to scan all around you. Then, your brain had to process the information and alert your hands to react to the information. These types of speed games, which involve quick scanning and focus matched with quick processing, are vital to a healthy brain.

Video games are one way that you can improve your mental health. While video games have gotten a bad reputation over the years for turning brains into mush, the opposite is true. Video games have been proven to increase multitasking abilities, focus, long-term memory, hand-eye coordination, problem solving, and critical thinking. As video games are studied more, more and more neuroscientists are trying to figure out how to make them even healthier for the brain. One neuroscientist even thinks video games could one day be prescribed to those with dementia!

A Strong Sense of Purpose

One important part of developing a healthy brain is developing a sense of purpose. It has been shown that purpose gives you the drive to live a dynamic and complex life, giving you the motivation to do so. Later in life, those who have a purpose tend to live longer and experience less bouts of dementia than those who do not. Those without a purpose are more likely to succumb to dementia and depression.

Getting in the Flow

One popular term across many disciplines is the word "flow". Flow is the moment where you feel you are really with it, that your brain and body are jiving and you're ready to take on the world. In order to stay in the flow, we must practice mental acuity and learn what helps us get there. When we can find the times we were in the flow, we can find our purpose.

KEY TAKEAWAY: Cognitive reserve, the ability to constantly change and rewire the brain, is one of the most important factors in brain health. We can have high cognitive reserve by constantly discovering new things.

Chapter Six:
The Need for Sleep and Relaxation

Sleep is the most essential thing you can do to keep your body and mind in tip-top shape. Sleep is a natural reset of the brain, and it's not a passive phase. During sleep, your brain is healing and repairing itself, readying itself for a new day. All people need seven to eight hours of sleep a night, and those who say they can get by on less don't know what they're talking about. Sleep problems should not increase with age, so if you are having new-onset problems sleeping, it's time to see a doctor.

Sleep Medicine

Every person has a circadian rhythm that tells them when to sleep and when to rise. When we listen to our circadian rhythm, we also experience normal hunger pangs (pains) and develop a rhythm to our food intake as well. Listening to our circadian rhythm also enables us to stay healthy physically and have higher mental acuity.

One of the biggest threats to good sleep is a condition called sleep apnea, which affects about a quarter of men and 1/10th of all women. Sleep apnea is a condition where the body wakes slightly hundreds of times in the night, disrupting its natural rhythm and ability to repair the brain and rejuvenate the body for the next day.

A Well-Rested Brain Is A Healthy Brain

Sleep is an incredibly important factor in maintaining memory and heart health. For memory, sleep clears the hippocampus where short term memory and emotions are stored, and sorts the information into long-term memory so it can be accessed later. Studies have consistently found that when students are given text to memorize, those who had better sleep between the time of giving the information and performing the memory skill remembered more and did so more quickly.

In the case of heart health, studies have found that those who have had one coronary issue were much more likely to have another coronary issue without proper sleep. They were also more likely to develop diabetes if they didn't have enough sleep, which directly affects brain functioning, as we talked about in previous chapters.

The Rinse Cycle

You can think of sleep like the rinse cycle in your dishwasher or washing machine. Sleep is what washes the sludge off and enables the brain to clean itself so brain trash doesn't end up in your bloodstream.

Studies have also shown that dementia and sleep have a bi-directional relationship. The worse someone sleeps the more at risk they are for developing dementia. When dementia occurs, the person is also less likely to get good sleep. It's a vicious cycle.

The Top Ten Secrets to Slumber

There are ten things you can do to get a better night's sleep.

First, stick to a schedule and avoid long naps. Keep your circadian rhythm in rhythm, even during holidays and weekends.

Second, don't be a night owl. Sleep when it's dark out and stay awake when it's light out.

Third, wake up to early morning light. Expose your eyes to sunlight first thing in the morning to help set your body count.

Fourth, get moving and do regular physical activity.

Fifth, watch what you eat and drink. Avoid caffeine after lunch, and don't eat or drink for three hours before bed.

Sixth, mind your medicines. Stay away from pharmaceuticals.

Seventh, keep your bedroom cool, quiet, and dark. This helps keep your room conducive to proper sleep.

Eighth, eliminate electronics. Move electronics out of your bedroom and out of your sleeping space to get rid of blue light.

Ninth, establish bedtime rituals and stick to them. This gives your body cues to begin to calm down.

Tenth, know the warning signs of sleep disorders, like having trouble falling asleep or staying asleep three times a week, snoring frequently, and persistent daytime sleepiness.

Don't Forget Daytime R&R

There are quite a few ways to also get rest and relaxation during the day, which only aids in brain health. The most common ways are meditation, deep breathing, and mindfulness. These methods focus on slowing the body down and allowing you to sort what is in your brain in a meaningful way. These methods teach you how to think, how to rid yourself of emotional sludge, and how to create a healthier brain. Studies have found that people who engage in methods such as these are less likely to experience cognitive decline than those who do not.

Here are some other things that can help you build a more resilient and productive brain:

- Become a regular volunteer in your community.
- Express gratitude.
- Practice the art of forgiveness.
- Look for things that make you laugh.
- Take breaks from email and social media.
- Find another hour in your day at least once a week.
- Establish a system of rewards.
- Don't multitask—tackle your day like a surgeon.
- Identify your marbles and sand and plan accordingly.
- Declutter your life.
- Set aside fifteen minutes each day for yourself.
- Let yourself daydream.

- Do not be afraid to seek help from health professionals if you have concerns about your mental health.

Life's Transitions

Researchers have found that most people are happiest when they are very young and very old, with a dip during midlife. This is because older and younger people both tend to develop less stress than those in their midlife, who have stresses from work and parenting. Learning to manage stress during life transitions is the key to maintaining a sense of mental acuity and brain health.

KEY TAKEAWAY: Sleep is an incredibly important part of managing stress and helping the brain stay healthy. In addition to sleep, one must also find ways of relaxing and resting during the day as well.

Chapter Seven:
Food for Thought

Everyone knows that a good diet plays a vital role in how well you function, your lifestyle, and your brain health. There are multitudes of diets that are out in the world, each promoting different foods and telling you to stay away from others. However, most of these diets are created by people who don't truly understand nutrition—and don't understand you. Our doctors are not often telling us what we need to know during our appointments, so we must focus on getting information elsewhere—which could lead to problems.

The truth is that everyone's diet is different because everyone's chemical makeup is different. The best diet for you to follow is the one that is healthiest for your body and takes into account your allergies and sensitivities.

However, most studies have concluded that a Mediterranean diet, made mostly of fish, greens, nuts, oils, and olives, is most beneficial to both physical and mental health. However, it's important that when we focus on what we are eating, we focus on what we can eat as a permissive diet, not on what we can't eat. To this end, the MIND diet was created.

The MIND diet combines the Mediterranean diet with what's best for the brain. The short of the mind diet is that it's thumbs up to vegetables (particularly leafy greens), poultry, fish, olive oil, olives, and nuts, while thumbs down to butter, cheese, fried foods, and margarine.

What's Good for The Heart is Good for the Brain

One of the most important things we have learned is that a heart-healthy diet is also a brain-healthy diet. A heart healthy diet is one that enables the heart to work optimally. Because the heart pumps blood, a heart healthy diet increases the chance that the brain-blood barrier will work properly and allows the brain to get the nutrients it needs to perform optimally.

In addition to this, we must understand that different foods are superpowers to different people. Eating well looks different for everyone based on how their bodies react to the foods within them. We must learn to recognize our own ways of "eating well" to fully understand how to eat optimally for our health.

One way of eating that will help ensure your diet is full of good foods is rainbow eating. Trying to get each of the seven colors on your plate throughout the day practically ensures you're getting a variety of healthy and good foods in your body.

My Guide to Good Eating

One of the easiest ways to make sure you are eating well is to follow the "SHARP" protocol. The SHARP protocol uses five different steps to make sure we are eating well.

S stands for "slash the sugar and stick to your ABCs". By reducing sugar intake, we allow our blood sugar to stabilize and decrease

42

our risk of diabetes. We can do this by sticking to the ABCs. The A-list, the B-list, and the C-list of which foods should be eaten. The A-list foods are ones that are quality, the B-list foods are ones that we should include, and C-list foods are ones we should limit. A-list foods include fresh vegetables, whole berries, fish and seafood, healthy fats, and nuts and seeds. B-list foods include beans and legumes, whole fruits, low sugar and low-fat dairy, poultry, and whole grains. C-list foods to limit include fried foods, pastries and sugary foods, processed foods, red meat and red meat products, and whole-fat dairy high in saturated fat such as cheese and butter, and salt.

H stands for "hydrate smartly" by drinking water. When you feel hungry, it is smart to hydrate with water before eating.

A stands for "add more Omega-3 fatty acids from dietary sources." This basically means eat more fish and oils.

R stands for "reduce portions". Start with smaller portions of foods you're eating so that you can keep your body from taking in more calories than it really needs.

P stands for "plan ahead". Don't resort to nighttime decisions about what you're eating. That's a surefire way to end up eating crap, or going through the fast-food establishments. Instead, plan ahead and let yourself come up with nutritious meals so that when you're hungry, they're on hand.

Organic

Eating organic is not essential, as long as you know how to properly wash and clean your produce to rid it of pesticides and other toxins. However, eating grass-fed beef is important as it's healthier for you than commercially fed beef.

Spice It Up!

Spices, particularly turmeric, also have incredible benefits. Not only do they add flavor to a dish which allows you to enjoy eating it more and to not grow tired of it, but they also have health benefits for your brain by increasing the production of tau and other healthy chemicals in your cranium.

The Gluten Debate

A gluten-free diet is all the rage, and is the subject of a lot of documentaries, podcasts, books, and medical studies. However, a gluten-free diet is only needed for someone who has celiacs disease or celiac sensitivity. For these people, cutting gluten is essential. For the rest of us, we only need to be careful to choose gluten products carefully, eliminating the ones that are mixed with sugars, oils, and fats.

A last word of warning when it comes to diet: make sure you floss! Flossing removes the mouth of food debris and bacteria, and it allows for us to make sure we are not getting gum disease, which leads to inflammation.

KEY TAKEAWAY: A healthy heart diet is healthy for the brain as well. We should all strive to eat good, nutritious foods.

Chapter Eight:
Connection for Protection

Social connection is a vital part of brain health and emotional health. Studies have shown that widowers are 42% more likely to face mortality for six months after their spouse's death than non-widowers. This is because the social connection that married people experience is cut short. The loneliness and isolation lead to depression and despondency and a lower level of adequate sleep and nutrition, all which couple together to cause problems for someone's health.

In addition, researchers have found that children who were isolated when they were young had poorer health habits 20 years later, regardless of how the other factors improved. Isolation triggers the pain sensors in your brain in the same way physical pain does, which means that the body responds out of stress, sending cortisol racing through the bloodstream. As we learned earlier, cortisol affects physical health, particularly heart and brain health, in significant ways.

The Secret Sauce to a Long, Sharp Life

People who are lonely experience less happiness than others, which causes motivation and purpose to decline, as well as physical health and brain functioning.

Each of these studies show that it's not the number of relationships you have that matters, but the quality of the relationships you have. One close friend is much more significant to overall health than a wide circle of friends you can't count on.

Social media can get a bad reputation when it comes to loneliness and connection, however, social media can also be a tool for good. Social media allows users to keep up with other friends, thoughtfully listen and respond to what they put out there, and engage in dialogue. Research shows that adults who use social media the correct way—by becoming more closely connected with true friends—performed 25% better on cognitive tests than those who didn't.

It's important to find ways to connect with other human beings, whether it's by walking, joining a club, having a phone conversation, or doing an activity together. Connection with others is essential.
In addition, appropriate touch is also a very simple way of communicating with others. Hugs and other physical forms of affection often lift our spirits and provide the rush of brain chemicals we need to respond to loneliness.

KEY TAKEAWAY: Human connection is increasingly important as we age to remain physically and mentally healthy.

Chapter Nine:
Putting It All Together

In the next twelve weeks, we will focus on achieving five important goals: moving more throughout the week, finding new ways to stimulate the brain, prioritizing getting restful and routine sleep, introducing a new way to nourish your body, and connecting authentically with others and maintaining a vibrant social life.

Weeks One and Two

The first two weeks, you need to dive into the five ways to better help your brain health. The first is to begin to move more. Find new ways to incorporate movement and daily exercise into your routine so you can have the benefit of a healthy body and brain.

The second is to find a class you can take either online or in person, or find a new book to do or activity to take up to enhance your learning and discovery.

Third, develop better sleep hygiene by timing your eating habits and being honest about how much sleep you get and how much sleep you need. Develop a strong sleep habit.

Fourth, eat when the sun is up—and only when the sun is up! Remember to be SHARP about what you eat—slash sugar, hydrate properly, add omega-3s, reduce portions, and plan your meals accordingly.

For breakfast, eliminate the American breakfasts of sugar-laden smoothies and Frappuccino's, or high-fat breads and muffins and stick to cleaner meals like frittatas and omelets yogurts, or whole-grain oatmeal.

For lunch, try swapping out your fast food and sweet drinks for a salad, or a protein-rich lunch. Swap out your drinks for water or unsweetened tea.

For dinner, stick with the same kind of foods as lunch, and stay away from fast food. Add a glass of red wine if you'd like!

Lastly, connect with people. Think of someone you haven't spoken to in a while and invite them over for dinner.

Weeks 3 and 4

Add more to your new routine by choosing at least two of the following options:

- Go for a twenty-minute power walk.
- Invite a neighbor over for dinner.
- Have at least two meals with fish.
- Download a mediation app.
- Try to eliminate soft drinks from your diet.

Weeks 5 and 6

Choose at least three of the following options to add to your routine:

50

- Start a gratitude journal.
- Add fifteen more minutes to your exercise routine.
- Try yoga or Pilates.
- Avoid processed foods.
- Add a relaxing activity to your bedtime routine.

Weeks 7 and 8

Add more to your routine by doing each of the five following things:

- Look for opportunities to volunteer.
- Explore your local farmers' market and buy fresh foods.
- Schedule a checkup with your doctor if you haven't had one this year.
- Write a handwritten letter to a younger loved one and pass down a lesson.
- Read a book in one subject or genre that interests you but you're not used to reading.

Weeks 9 and 10

For weeks nine and ten, stop and note how you are doing in each of the five areas. For ones you are struggling with, go back and reread the sections in this book to learn more and find a new focus.

Weeks 11 and 12

For week 11, think about how you would want your children or other family members to deal with a dementia or Alzheimer's diagnosis. Write these wishes down and speak with your family about them so you and they can be prepared going forward.

Now that you're in week 12, take some time to really study what you've done over the past few weeks. What has worked and what hasn't? Also study your motivation. How can you make the next 12 weeks even better than the last 12 weeks?

KEY TAKEAWAY: In order to better yourself in 12 weeks, follow the guidelines to create actionable steps in each of the five main areas.

Part Three:
The Diagnosis: What to Do and How To Thrive

Chapter Ten:
Diagnosing and Treating an Ailing Brain

For most people, the idea of losing their memory is incredibly frightening. More people are afraid of Alzheimer's Disease than any other disease in America. Bill Gates, millionaire and founder of Microsoft, is one of those people and has invested millions of dollars in dementia and Alzheimer's research. The problem with Alzheimer's is that everyone wants a cure—but they want the cure to come after Alzheimer's has already set in. Alzheimer's begins in as early as your 30s with the buildup of amyloids and tau, so by the time you show symptoms decades later, it's already entrenched in your body. Therefore, in order to effectively 'cure' Alzheimer's, we must start much earlier with prevention.

Bringing Hope

Sandy Halperin is an Alzheimer's sufferer who has used his diagnosis to bring awareness to the disease and to promote funding and decreased shame associated with memory loss. Halperin, like many other seniors, began feeling the effects of his memory loss several years before he was diagnosed. He is a strong advocate for people not waiting to get diagnosed, since, by the time they are diagnosed with Alzheimer's, the disease is already so entrenched that every second counts. Halperin experiences short moments of lucidity.

A Pound of Prevention

Dr. Isaacson is one of the leading doctors on memory and cognition. Isaacson realized early that an ounce of prevention is worth a pound of cure, and sought to develop a program that would help prevent diseases such as Alzheimer's and conditions like dementia from occurring more rapidly. While there is no cure for either, his programs do account for a delay of roughly three years, making the brain seem younger than it is and slowing the onset of memory-related illnesses.

His program follows the ABC method, where A stands for anthropometrics, like body mass and fat percentage, B stands for blood biomarkers, such as cholesterol, and C stands for cognitive performance to test for memory functioning and recall. He begins by testing patients on the ABCs and then develops a personalized plan for them to follow, re-testing and adjusting the plan every six months.

There are three stages of Alzheimer's Disease: early (mild), middle (moderate), and late (severe). These three stages can impact how a person receives treatment, and like cancer, how likely they are to live past a certain time. The average life expectancy for someone diagnosed with Alzheimer's is 4-8 years, though some have lived as

54

long as 20 years after diagnosis. The problem is that most people are not being diagnosed until after they have already entered the latest stages.

Early Stage: Mild Alzheimer's Disease

The early stage of Alzheimer's is often referred to as mild cognitive decline, and it can often be mistaken for forgetfulness or aloofness. For those in this stage, they may find they forget familiar faces or places, that they experience mood changes and social withdrawal, they struggle to communicate and have difficulty with their vision, and they show poor planning skills, judgment, or decision-making skills.

Middle Stage: Moderate Alzheimer's Disease

The moderate stage of Alzheimer's is the longest lasting, and provides a steep change. In this stage, Alzheimer's patients may find themselves wandering or lost, they may have trouble controlling their bladder or sleeping, become suspicious of those around them, or need help with simple tasks like choosing an outfit for the day.

Late Stage: Severe Alzheimer's Disease

Late-stage Alzheimer's patients are almost unable to communicate, and find themselves only experiencing very small moments of lucidity.

It is difficult to receive an Alzheimer's diagnosis because there is not only one test to be taken in order to determine someone has the disease. Rather, the disease is diagnosed after observation, coupled with MRIs, CT, and PET scans. None of these tests show definitively that someone does have Alzheimer's, but are rather used to eliminate other potential causes and rule out diseases that could have similar symptoms.

Dementia Mimics

Normal pressure hydrochephalus (NPH) is a neurological disorder that causes dementia. However, this disorder can be improved upon. NPH is characterized by walking abnormalities and impaired bladder control. It's caused by a buildup of cerebrospinal fluid in the brain. It's been found that draining some of the fluid from the brain can help with these symptoms.

Another factor in dementia is medication. On average, Americans take five different medications ranging from sleep aids to anxiety relief to opiates to blood pressure medicine. These medications, as you grow, affect the body more and more. This is why it's essential that you always tell your doctors every medication you're taking.

Drugs that have been known to increase susceptibility to dementia are anticholinergic antidepressants (paroxetine, Paxil), anti Parkinson's drugs and antihistamines (Benadryl), antipsychotic drugs, and anti epileptic drugs.

Depression is another disorder that can make dementia worse, and can even look like dementia. Depression is often referred to as psuedo-dementia because the symptoms of depression (moodiness, social withdrawal, low emotional regulation, fuzzy memory) are also often associated with dementia. In addition, depression can lead to increased risk for dementia, and dementia has been shown to increase the chances of depression, as well.

Urinary tract infections (UTI) can also lead to memory fogginess, confusion, delirium, and other symptoms that look similar to dementia.

Vascular dementia is brain damage that is caused by multiple strokes, and causes memory loss in older adults. It can also cause difficulties with cognitive reasoning and judgment, as well as memory.

Nutritional deficiencies, particularly of B12 and niacin, can also lead to memory issues and fogginess. Deficiencies are rare in the Western world, however, and can be remedied through diet and supplementation.

Infections such as syphilis and Lyme disease can also make you more prone to dementia. Any vector-borne ailments can impact the brain and memory.

One of the more obvious dementia-related conditions could be a benign brain tumor. Brain tumors take up space in the brain, blocking neural pathways and adding pressure.

A subdural hematoma, a result of trauma to the brain, can also show signs of dementia and lead to it. Traumatic brain injury causes the brain to become inflamed. It ends up tearing bridging veins that cross the subdural space. This can be something as small as knocking your head on a car door, and can show up even weeks later.

Alcohol-related dementia can also cause long-term problems for those who have a history of alcohol consumption. Alcohol, particularly combined with other drugs and medications, can exasperate memory issues and changes in mood.

Anyone who has concerns over whether they may be experiencing Alzheimer's or not should contact their doctor for a full medical workup. This will include a physical, cognitive scans, observation, and other tests that are used to check the cognitive level of the participant. Generally speaking, after all of this has been done a medical made up of a neurologist, psychiatrist, and psychologist will assess the results and help you assess the disease.

Nationwide Programs: Where to Find Help

It may seem overwhelming to face an Alzheimer's diagnosis, but there is a lot of help out there for people who have experienced memory loss, dementia, and ultimately, Alzheimer's. Some of the places one can go for help are: AARP, the Alzheimer's Association, The Cleveland Clinic's Lou Ruvo Center for Brain Health, The Dementia Action Alliance, The Family Caregiver Alliance, The Mayo Clinic's Alzheimer's Disease Research Center, The Memory Disorders Program at the New York-Presbyterian/Weill Cornell Medical

Center, The National Institute on Aging Funds Alzheimer's Disease Research Centers, and the UCLA's Alzheimer's and Dementia Care Programs.

The Future

Early detection and treatment of Alzheimer's is key. Not only does early detection mean that the disease isn't as entrenched in your brain once you start treatment, but it also means that you may be more eligible for clinical trials that could increasingly impact your ability to care for yourself and others.

Treatments: Drug-Based and People-Based

There are two types of therapy that are prescribed to Alzheimer's patients to help them with their symptoms: drug therapy and human therapy.

Drug therapy includes a cocktail of two different kinds of drugs, cholinesterase inhibitors and NMDA receptor antagonists. These drugs are often prescribed in the later stages of Alzheimer's, and they work together to improve brain functionality and aim to restore it to earlier levels. Of course, they are not a cure for Alzheimer's and while they are somewhat effective, they are by no means a saving grace.

The other prescription is a human-based therapy, which involves a dedicated caregiver to the person suffering. Many doctors believe that a good caretaker is worth even more than drugs to a late-stage Alzheimer's patient.

KEY TAKEAWAY: There are many different signs to look out for to know if you are experiencing Alzheimer's symptoms, and it's helpful to rule out other potential causes of memory loss.

Chapter Eleven:
Navigating the Path Forward Financially, and Emotionally with a Special Note to Caregivers

One of the most challenging things about navigating Alzheimer's disease for families is figuring out what should be done to ensure the patient is safe. Long-term care facilities are incredibly expensive, especially for people who are experiencing late-stage Alzheimer's and need around-the-clock care. Not providing a caregiver is incredibly dangerous, but asking a family member to step in is taxing emotionally and financially. Many families are left wondering where they should turn.

It Takes a Village

One of the most interesting places in the world is Hogewyek, a Dutch village that has been deemed "Dementia Village". Hogewyek is a beautiful village designed to help those with Alzheimer's by mimicking real life in a safe way and allowing them to have traces of normalcy. The village is on four acres, and each of the residents lives in a dormitory-style house with their own bedrooms. These houses are made to resemble houses they would have lived in when they were younger—the wealthy have ornate houses, immigrants have houses that look like their culture, etc. Each house is equipped with trained staff who help the residents do their washing and cooking.

Outside of the house there is an entire village, complete with a grocery store, cafes and restaurants, and different activities. Residents are free to wander anywhere they wish, and there is ample security to make sure they are doing so safely. There is only one door in and out of the facility, and if a member becomes confused and tries to exit, they're told that the door doesn't work.

When visiting this location, a conversation with one of the staff was enlightening. She said to never tell a dementia person they are confused or to correct them, but to instead ask probing questions. If a person with dementia claims it's time for dinner when they just ate, you could ask them if they are hungry. If they claim their parents are still alive, ask them how old they are. Let them come to conclusions on their own.

Brace Yourself

The average caretaker in the United States is a middle-aged female. Usually, this is the daughter or granddaughter of someone with an ailment. Often, this person also has children of their own, which only increases the level of stress.

Many caregivers report that they are more stressed when they are caring for both children and their elderly parents or grandparents. These caregivers report that they never feel they are staying ahead of the problems and that they are drowning in them. In order to help with this issue, it's essential that caregivers find other means of support for themselves and those who need care. By contacting other family members and friends, they can relieve part of the burden.

The other major burden facing caregivers is financial. An Alzheimer patient's treatment costs around $11,000 annually, and this comes out of the pocket of the patient and her family. Many worry that they won't be able to meet this financial burden, and that what they meant to save for their children and grandchildren will be no more by the time they are done.

It is important for caregivers to look for social-connection services in their areas, as well as trials, financial help and grants. Those affected with Alzheimer's should also make a financial plan for their care, develop a care team, and make efforts to ensure their homes are safe for them with added security measures.

Keep Talking

It's essential that everyone, not just those with dementia-related illness, make these same types of plans. Everyone should have a financial plan and a care team plan set in place that their families can use as a guideline to follow. Without one, families may disagree on what steps need to be taken and it can tear the family apart. In certain cases, it may even be necessary to get a conservatorship, which is when an outside party comes in to take control, leaving the family helpless.

The Invisible Second Patient

One statistic that is frightening is that caregivers of those with dementia are six times more likely to develop dementia than others. This is because they are surrounded by it, isolated from others around them, and overcome with stress. As we talked about earlier, high levels of cortisol (the stress hormone) in the blood can mean that we experience toxicity in the brain and can also lead to larger amyloid and tau growth, the leading causes of dementia. In order to beat this statistic, caregivers of those with dementia must find ways to relieve their stress.

Don't Forget Yourselves: A Note to Caregivers

Caregivers must learn how to take care of themselves by adopting healthy practices such as good nutrition, exercise, and meditation practices. In doing so, they can help prevent caregiver burnout and help themselves become more present and healthy as they are caring for those around them.

Two of the biggest causes of burnout for a caregiver are actually emotions. The feelings of guilt and dealing with denial often cause an immense emotional burden on caregivers. Those around them may deny that the problem is as bad as it is, and they may question the caregiver's decisions, thinking they know better. In addition, the caregiver may feel guilty for not providing more direct care, or for being overwhelmed by the problem at hand.

It is essential that caregivers take care of themselves and that they find support from those around them. AARP and the Alzheimer's Association both have networks that can help connect caregivers to one another, as well as offering research, remedies, tricks and other ways to support caregivers as they care for those ailing from Alzheimer's.

KEY TAKEAWAY: It is emotionally and financially stressful to care for those with Alzheimer's. Caregivers must do everything they can to make sure they do not fall victim to burnout.

Background Information About
Dr. Sanjay Gupta

Dr. Sanjay Gupta is a three-time New York Times bestselling author and the chief medical correspondent for CNN. He has been the CNN national correspondent since 2001, covering the effects of terrorism attacks on the health of first responder, natural disease outbreaks, and the effects of drugs on Americans. He has received multiple Emmy and Peabody awards, as well as the DuPont award. He has also written two nonfiction books and is widely regarded as one of the media's most trusted reporters.

In 2019, Gupta was elected to the National Academy of Medicine, one of the medical fields' highest honors. He lives in Atlanta, Georgia, and is a professor of neurosurgery at Emory University Hospital and the associate chief of neurosurgery at Grady Memorial Hospital.

Trivia Questions

1. What are the three steps in memory creation?
2. What is CTE and what does it tell us about brain functioning?
3. What are the five pillars of brain health?
4. How much exercise is recommended per week, and what kind of exercise?
5. What are the ten steps to getting better sleep?
6. What are the five areas we must improve in for better brain health?

Discussion Questions

1. In chapter three we read about the 12 myths about the brain. Are there any you have believed and were surprised to know weren't true?

2. When was the last time you were able to get rest and relaxation like what was discussed in chapter six?

3. How can you change your diet so that you are giving your brain the best chance to be healthy?

4. Referring to the 12-week program outlined in chapter nine, what can you do to make sure that you are successful while implementing the plan for a better brain?

THANK YOU FOR FINISHING THE BOOK!

Looks like you've enjoyed it! :)

We here at Cosmic Publications will always strive to deliver to you the highest quality guides. So, I'd like to thank you for supporting us and reading until the very end.

Before you go, would you mind leaving us a review on Amazon? It will mean a lot to us and support us creating high quality guides for you in the future. Just scan the QR code below.

Thank you again.

Warmly,

The Cosmic Publications Team

Summary Guides you might also enjoy.

Manufactured by Amazon.ca
Bolton, ON